48/200.

"S

CW00867899

| Bill Hickie

First Printing: 2014

ISBN 978-1-291-75570-1

www.stop-pressing-snooze.com

| Bill Hickie

Contents

| Bill Hickie

I'd like to introduce three simple, different and important behaviours that we are all very familiar with, I call them the "3 P's".

"Procrastination, Pro-Activity & Productivity"

The "3 P's" are inextricably linked. Avoiding procrastination leads to having a pro-active can do mind-set, enabling you to produce exponentially. Thinking about the "3 P's" enabled me to write this book and more importantly bring three innocuous words together that changed my life forever...

"Stop Pressing Snooze!"

How many times has your alarm gone off, you look at the time, think of the tasks ahead, look at the time again and then press the snooze button. It's so easy; it feels so right, it can't be wrong. Don't be fooled....it is wrong.

It's wrong because, you set that alarm, you made than plan to get up, but you didn't make it, you didn't do it, you gave up. That behaviour of putting off the inevitable, taking the easy route and seeking temporary satisfaction becomes habitual. Things never get done, life passes you by. Don't let that be you.

"Stop Pressing Snooze!"

Three simple words you will never forget.

Stop Pressing Snooze breaks the habits, and provides 100 anecdotes, tips and tools to help eradicate the debilitating behaviours linked to procrastination and, in-turn, poor productivity.

Take the first step and start the change.

**"the act of procrastinating;
putting off, delaying or deferring
an action to a later time"**

One of the most common problems in life is procrastination. We know what we want to do and what we should do but we still end up spending hours upon hours doing "easier" work or escaping via TV, social networking or music.

Of course, it's absolutely essential that you take time out to relax, but if you procrastinate too much you don't get the most important things done.

Procrastination is fostered by habit. So if you want to stop procrastinating, you have to break old habits and develop new ones. Try to understand the causes for your procrastination. If you can, you're halfway there. Recognise the difference between an appropriate decision to delay and an irrational postponement without justification.

"Only put off until tomorrow what you are willing to die having left undone"

Pablo Picasso

1.   The First Step.

To overcome procrastination you need to have an understanding of the reasons why you procrastinate and the function procrastination serves in your life. You can't come up with an effective solution if you don't really understand the root of the problem. As with most problems, awareness and self-knowledge are the keys to figuring out how to stop procrastinating. When you are tempted to fall into familiar, unproductive, procrastinating habits, ask yourself Why? This goes a long way to solving the problem.

2.   Break your work into little steps.

Part of the reason we procrastinate is because subconsciously, we find the work too overwhelming for us. Break it down into little parts, then focus on one part at the time. If you still procrastinate on the task after breaking it down, then break it down even further. Focus on the immediate phase and get it done to your best ability, without thinking about the other phases. When it's done, move on to the next.

                | Bill Hickie

3.   Change your environment.

Different environments have different effects on our productivity. Look at your desk and your office or office space. Do they make you want to work or do they make you want to relax or worse sleep? If it's the latter, you should look into changing your workspace. In addition, an environment that makes us feel inspired before may lose its effect after a period of time. If that's the case, then it's time to change things around and revamp your environment.

4.   Create a detailed timeline with specific deadlines.

Having just one deadline for your work is like an invitation to procrastinate. That's because we get the impression that we have time and keep pushing everything back, until it's too late. Break down your project, then create an overall timeline with specific deadlines for each small task. This way, you know you have to finish each task by a certain date. This also creates the urgency to act.

5.   Spend time with people who inspire you.

How can you soar like an eagle if you are surrounded by turkeys. The people we are with, influence our behaviours. Identify the people, friends & colleagues who trigger you – most likely the high achievers and hard workers – and spend more time with them. Soon you will absorb their drive and spirit too.

6.   Find a Friend.

Having a companion makes the whole process much more fun. Ideally, your friend should be someone who has their own set of goals. Both of you will hold each other accountable to your goals and plans. While it's not necessary for both of you to have the same goals, it'll be even better if that's the case, so you can learn from each other. I have a number of good friends whom I talk to regularly, and we always ask each other about our goals and progress in achieving those goals. Needless to say, it spurs us to keep taking action.

7.   Tell others about your goals.

Tell all your friends, colleagues, acquaintances and family about your projects. Now whenever you see them, they are bound to ask you about your status on those projects. It's a great way to keep yourself accountable to your plans.

8.   Seek out someone who has already achieved the outcome.

What is it you want to accomplish here, and who are the people who have accomplished this already? Seek them out and connect with them. Seeing living proof that your goals are very well achievable if you take action is one of the best triggers for action.

© Stop-Pressing-Snooze | Bill Hickie

9.   Re-clarify your goals.

If you have been procrastinating for an extended period of time, it might reflect a misalignment between what you want and what you are currently doing. Often we outgrow our goals as we discover more about ourselves, but we don't change our goals to reflect that. Get away from your work and take some time to regroup yourself. What exactly do you want to achieve? What should you do to get there? What are the steps to take? Does your current work align with that? If not, what can you do about it?

10.   Stop over-complicating things.

Are you waiting for a perfect time to do this? That maybe now is not the best time because of certain reasons? There's never a perfect time. If you keep waiting for one, you are never going to accomplish anything. Perfectionism is one of the biggest reasons for procrastination.

11.   Get a grip.

At the end of the day, it boils down to taking action. You can do all the strategising & planning in the world but if you don't take action, nothing's going to happen. No-one can procrastinate their way to success. Whatever it is you are procrastinating on, if you want to get it done, you need to get a grip and just do it.

12.   Stop thinking & Start doing.

A bit of planning can certainly help you to achieve what you want to achieve. A lot of planning and thinking tends to have the opposite effect. Stop trying to come up with "the perfect plan", a plan where you don't have to make mistakes, where you will never be rejected, where there will be no pain or difficulties. Such a thing does not exist.

13.   Don't blow a task out of proportion.

By over thinking and putting things off you make mountains out of molehills. The more hours and days you put something off the worse it grows in your mind. And since you are putting it off you are probably thinking about it in a negative way. So plan a little and then take action. Often you don't even have to plan, you have been there before and you know what needs to be done.

             | Bill Hickie

14.   Just take the first step.

When you start to look too far into the future any task or project can seem close to impossible, and you shut down because you become overwhelmed. That is one of the reasons why it is good to plan for the future but then to shift your focus back to today and the present moment. Just focus on taking the first step today. That is all you need to focus on, nothing else. By taking the first step you change your mental state from resistant to pro-active. You put yourself in a state where you become more positive and open, a state where you may not be enthusiastic about taking the next step after this first one but you are at least accepting it. And so you can take the next step. And the next one after that.

15.   Start with the hardest task of your day.

Maybe you have an important call to make that you also fear may be uncomfortable. Maybe you know you have fallen behind on answering your emails and have a lot of work to do. Whatever it may be, get it out of your way first. If you start your day this way you will feel relieved. You feel relaxed and good about yourself. And the rest of the day – and your to-do list – tends to feel a lot lighter and easier to move through. It's amazing what difference this one action makes.

© Stop-Pressing-Snooze | Bill Hickie

16. Just make a decision.

We feel bad when we sit on our hands and don't take action because it's unnatural. The natural thing is to be a decisive human and take action. When you procrastinate you want to do something but you don't take the action. You become conflicted within. What you do always sends signals back to yourself about who you are. Taking the confident actions you want to take over and over again is what really builds your self confidence and a self-image of you being a confident person. When you procrastinate you lower your self-esteem. Don't do it.

17. Face your fear.

Avoid your comfort zone. The easy choice can come with a sense of comfort and a certain level of success but also pangs of regret for all the things you never dared to do and a vague sense of being unfulfilled. You wonder about what would have happened if you had taken more action and more chances. The harder choice gives you, well, who knows? But it will make your feel more alive. Embrace Life.

     | Bill Hickie

18.   Finish it.

Not taking the first step to start accomplishing something can make you feel bad. But not finishing what you have started can also leave you in a negative mind set. You feel fatigued or stressed and sometimes you don't even know why. If that is the case, go over tasks and projects that you are currently involved in. Is there something there you know you want to finish but haven't yet? Try to get that finished as soon as you can and you will start to feel a whole lot better. Just be careful. Don't think you have to finish everything you started. Sometimes finishing the first part is good enough.

19.   It's not as bad as you think.

Unpleasant tasks rarely turn out to be as bad as you think. Complete these tasks first. Schedule them for early in the day. Give yourself a reward for doing them.

20.   Make up your mind.

People delay because they can't make up their minds. Determine a time for making a decision and the criteria for making it. Share your deadline with someone else.

© Stop-Pressing-Snooze | Bill Hickie

21.   Don't fear failure.

People don't want to face the consequences of failure, so they delay. Develop a clear mental picture of the completed task and how you will feel at that time. Maintain a focus on the end result, not just the process. Remind yourself how good you'll feel when you're finished.

22.   Get interested.

You are tired or lazy. You' re just not very interested in the task. Reward yourself for accomplishments. Go out for special lunches when major projects are completed. If you don't earn the reward, don't take it.

23.   The problem with perfectionism.

People delay because they want to get the project perfect. Set deadlines for yourself. Maintain your high standards, but recognise that sometimes 80% for you may well be 100% for someone else. Don't spend hours conducting a detailed cost breakdown when a rough estimate would suffice.

24.   Remove hostility in the workplace.

People delay because they don't like the person who assigned the task. Review with your boss what exactly is needed. Clarify the expectations. Be SMART with objectives.

          | Bill Hickie

25.   Get focussed.

Sometimes losing concentration causes delays. Create a to-do list with priorities. Block your time for projects. As you get distracted from a work project, make a rule that you are not allowed to move out of your chair, make a call, until you return to your task. Complete something. Make a very small task for yourself and finish it. Very small. Then, make another one.

26.   Understand the difference of delay.

Delay does not mean procrastinate. Procrastination is about indefinite postponement; delaying is about consciously rescheduling something for a more appropriate time. Delaying in this sense is actually proactive. You are choosing the best time to do something so that it works with your schedule, work style and priorities. Scan your list of to-dos and ask yourself: What absolutely doesn't have to happen today? Even if you've determined that a task is important, consider whether it can be postponed a day or a week to a more logical and practical time. Delaying sometimes requires that we fight our own impulse to gravitate toward tasks we enjoy or consider easy at the expense of more important, difficult ones. Delaying also involves resisting your tendency to instantly respond to requests from other people. Just because someone asks you to do something the moment they think of it doesn't mean it's urgent; perhaps they just wanted to get it off their own list.

© Stop-Pressing-Snooze | Bill Hickie

27. Avoid last minute dot com.

Once you know what the assignment is, get started on it. Procrastination will tempt you to put these assignments off until the last minute, but don't give into that temptation.

28. Start Tasks Without Thinking.

Instead of dipping your toe in the water to check the temperature, jump in. The same principle applies to starting work, instead of telling yourself you are going do it after you check your e-mail or after you drink your morning coffee or diet coke. Just go ahead and start it, you will see that in the process of completing work that there is nothing to fear about it, even if it's difficult. At least you're doing it.

29. If you are stuck ask.

Instead of wasting time wracking your brain, be humble and approach a colleague even if they are a subordinate. Say, "I'm running out of ideas, can you brainstorm with me?" or "I can't solve this problem. Maybe you see something in it that I don't?" Procrastinating in asking for help won't solve anything, but swallowing your pride can yield tremendous benefits. It makes your colleague feel good, and they can offer a fresh perspective on the problem.

 | Bill Hickie

30.　Boost your Willpower.

Willpower is like a muscle. You can exhaust it more quickly than you might imagine and, when you do, you lose your ability to self-regulate your behaviour. One immediate method to strengthen your resolve in order to keep you on task is to remind yourself of your values. This process of self-affirmation bolsters our flagging reserves of willpower.

31.　Leverage Anxiety.

Too much anxiety is paralysing. But a little anxiety is motivating. Learn to gauge your anxiety level. If it's too high, and you're procrastinating because you're simply overwhelmed by it, get professional help to manage it. Don't be ashamed.

32.　Visualise goals.

Focus on what you want to do, not what you want to avoid. Think about the productive reasons for doing a task by setting positive, concrete, meaningful learning and achievement goals for yourself.

33.　Be Realistic.

Achieving goals and changing habits takes time and effort; don't sabotage yourself by having unrealistic expectations that you cannot reasonably meet.

　　　© Stop-Pressing-Snooze　　　| Bill Hickie

| Bill Hickie

"serving to prepare for, intervene in, or control an expected occurrence or situation, especially against a negative or difficult one"

Being proactive means planning, thinking and acting ahead. It's a great method for avoiding unnecessary work in the future and can also be extremely important for averting disasters. Pro-activity also makes you more attractive. Many of us look to proactive people as the instigators of action and creative ideas in society.

Don't get so caught up in planning that you fail to act – "paralysis by analysis". A plan does not need to be watertight, only indicative and motivating. You can always return to it as time goes on and add more. There is no such thing as perfection and trying to reach this at the commencement of a plan is wasted effort. Flexibility is a key positive trait of a proactive person. Being proactive means anticipating and preparing for all possible outcomes, not controlling your future.

"In a moment of decision, the best thing you can do is the right thing to do, the next best thing is the wrong thing, and the worst thing you can do is nothing."

Theodore Roosevelt

34.   Try to prevent problems from ever arising.

This means tackling possible failings in advance to prevent them from becoming a reality. Get into the habit of taking precautions and developing fall-back plans.

35.   Always carry a small notebook.

That way, if you are hit by an idea, you can quickly note it down. Afterwards when you read your notes, you will discover about 90% of your ideas are really stupid. Don't worry, that's normal. What's important are the 10% that are brilliant.

36.   Develop a can-do mind-set.

Here's how: Define the problem. Decide what needs to happen to overcome the problem and how you're going to do that. Get on with it.

37.   Get ahead.

The early bird catches the worm. Get to work early and clear your desks and tasks whilst it's quiet. Doing so means that they'll be out of the way when the rush comes and you will not be worrying you unnecessarily. A little effort up front could save you from a larger crisis later.

© Stop-Pressing-Snooze | Bill Hickie

38.   Eliminate waste.

Some things do not need doing, or do not need to be done by you. Do not waste time on them and do not allow a misplaced sense of guilt lead you into thinking that somehow you are responsible for them. Be ruthless in making this assessment about the value of a task.

39.   Evaluate and win.

What works and what does not? Make notes for improvements, and incorporate those improvements during the next lull. Discard anything that does not work but take care to note when something is in need of tweaking and adjust it accordingly so that it does work.

40.   Anticipate needs.

Are there extra activities associated with certain times of the day, week, month, or time of year? Can you prepare in advance? Look ahead and don't be afraid of the unknown. A small amount of future stability can be self-generated by planning ahead and being ready for those things over which you do have some control.

© Stop-Pressing-Snooze | Bill Hickie

41.   Find out what you need to know.

Can you learn a new skill ahead of time? Can you apply a skill you already have in a new way? Watch the trends around you; keep up-to-date by reading and continuous learning. Proactive people are successful because they are immersed in unfolding history as well as understanding the lessons of the past.

42.   Look to automate.

Computers can manipulate data in all sorts of ways. If you work in a team context, delegation is also a form of automation, in that knowing the best person to do a task will automatically result in its being done to the best level possible, removing it from the pile of "to-do's". Put in place a system that automatically moves tasks to those best suited to them.

43.   Learn something new.

Learn something just for the sake of learning something. Take up an interest. Develop a passion.

44.　Tell Yourself A Different Story.

It's not your boss or the deadline that's stressing you out. It's you, or rather, your reaction to it. It's the story you tell yourself about the stress that makes it stressful. Work stress is not a matter of life and limb, but your brain interprets it that way. The first thought after a stressful event is a distortion by the panicked brain, the amygdala. It's a false alarm. When the stress goes off and the emotions rage, step back, take a breath, and reframe the event with a different attitude. Stay neutral in this situation, don't let emotions run you, and dispute the stress with the facts of the situation.

45.　Get More Sleep.

High performers in any field need to be fully rested to be at the top of their game. Sleep is a critical engine of productivity that's often overlooked in the bravado of the workplace. If you don't get enough shut-eye your brain will be compromised. Sleep is essential to remember things, to connect data, and to help restore the body. Some people can get by on a few hours of sleep, but others may need a lot more to reach their basal sleep need. When you're not getting enough sleep, you build up a sleep deficit that has to be restored.

© Stop-Pressing-Snooze | Bill Hickie

46.   Plan Your Holidays.

Plan your holidays at least three months in advance and take all of them. Holidays are as important to your health as watching your cholesterol and getting exercise. Holidays away cure burnout, increase positive mood and boost productivity when you return. If you don't take vacations seriously and plan ahead, they either don't happen or you end up with a last-minute substitute, like idling around the house. Start planning at least three months in advance. Do your homework, and you'll have a chance to craft the best times of your life.

47.   Get Out Of Denial.

The bravado workplace makes you think it's weak to admit you're stressed. The reality is that real weakness comes from not admitting it, because what happens when you don't deal with stress or communicate about it is that you think about it, and accelerate the stress spiral and the catastrophic thoughts that come with it. Listen to your body for the stress signals; fatigue, insomnia, irritability, anxiety, lack of energy, difficulty concentrating, neck pain, back pain. Find out what's causing the stress, and resolve it.

 | Bill Hickie

48.   Man is like an I-Pod.

After three straight hours working on a task, the brain has reached its limit, and you have to get off task to recharge your mental batteries. We're no different than mobile phones or I-Pods. Take two 10 to 15 minute breaks in the morning and two in the afternoon to recharge yourself. Use the time to get away from the work mind and tap in to things you enjoy. Plan your weekend. Breaks interrupt stressors and rejuvenate brain cells. Consider these pauses as opportunities to pump up your day and prevent mental burn-outs.

49.   Control Obsessive Anxiety.

In business you have to be very good at understanding risk, which basically comes down to tolerating ambiguity. Withstanding uncertainty requires an ability to regularly get your anxiety down. One of the best tools for this is the relaxation response, also known as meditation. It's a fantastic tool for calming the mind and eliminating obsessive thinking. Try it.

© Stop-Pressing-Snooze | Bill Hickie

50.   Avoid Burnout.

The same traits that drive you to success can push you over the edge into chronic stress and the last stage of anxiety, Burnout. When you're burned out, your running on empty. All your resources have been depleted. It's a three-way shutdown, emotional, physical and mental. It's a serious condition that needs to be fixed immediately before it leads to something even worse. Changing schedules, reducing workload, increasing support, and making sure you get regular recharge time can keep burnout at bay. Recognise the signs of burnout; no sense of accomplishment, depersonalisation of others, lack of enjoyment, nothing left to give, depleted emotional resources, physical exhaustion and cynicism.

51.   Don't Overdo It.

It's not easy, but it's mandatory in a 24/7 world. Sometimes you have to say no. Sometimes you can't get it done when the client wants it done. Don't stretch yourself too thin, or get bogged down in low-value tasks that take you away from creating the revenue your business needs to survive otherwise you will end up being undermined by your own work ethic. You can't do it all effectively.

52.   Stop Thinking Of Time as an Unlimited Commodity.

Essentially, just as a cupboard is a limited space into which you must fit a certain number of objects, a schedule is a limited space into which you must fit a certain number of tasks. When you realise the actual limits of your time, you become much more selective about what you put into the "cupboard".

53.   Find A Hobby.

There's no better way to get the stress down than finding a passion or pursuit you can indulge on a regular basis. Facebook does not count as a hobby. Identify an activity you have an affinity for, maybe something you always wanted to do, like running a marathon or sign up for an activity class. Studies show a clear link between frequent participation in leisure activities and life satisfaction and stress reduction.

54.   Mark Your Spot When Getting Interrupted.

It takes at least 20 minutes to get back to the level of concentration that had been attained before a disruption. Leaving a "Next Action" Post-it can eliminate that reorientation time completely. If you need to stop in the middle of a project, make it easier to pick up where you left off by writing yourself a little "Next Action" note. On a brightly coloured Post-it, placed directly onto the document, indicate where you left off and write down the very step you need to take next. Investing a minute to mark your spot before you stop will save you time currently lost to getting reoriented.

© Stop-Pressing-Snooze

55.   Set Realistic Deadlines.

If you think you can get things done faster than you can, make sure to stop and reassess before you promise a delivery date you can't meet. Things always take longer than you think, and chronic over-promising is a huge and needless stressor. Build in time for scope creep, an extra 25 percent or more. Realistic deadlines mean saying no sometimes and proposing alternative scenarios. Your goal should be a time frame that is feasible for effective performance.

56.   Articulate Your Personal Vision.

Your career is a major part of your life. What drives you to be where you are? What, beyond this moment, keeps propelling you forward? What is the vision that inspires you? Take a minute now to articulate what drives you personally. State clearly what you are working toward. Developing a vision can be a little overwhelming, but it doesn't need to be complicated. What does your gut tell you? What do you want? What's making you wake up every day to get started on your work? Don't feel pressured to articulate your one-year, five-year, and 10-year goals. Vision is often as hard to describe as feeling an impulse, a wish or a desire. You may be driven to learn as much as you possibly can about your industry, or to develop a reputation as the best in your field. Maybe you want to be a role model for others. Often, your vision is a dream, a hope, or a belief in yourself and the unique contribution you can make to the world through your work. Whatever compels you, articulate it. It will grow stronger and more inspiring as you acknowledge and embrace it.

© Stop-Pressing-Snooze | Bill Hickie

57.   Keep an Eye on Your Physical Health.

Caffeine, sugar and the pure will to concentrate can compensate short term for lack of sleep and poor nutrition, but nothing substitutes for genuine physical health. Sleep, exercise, a proper diet and regular check-ups are important for maintaining your physical health. This is a basic, essential priority, which provides the well of energy from which you draw the strength to accomplish everything you need to do. Some people neglect their own health for so long that they forget what it feels like to be healthy and rested. Making the commitment to your physical health will have an immediately visible effect on your productivity.

58.   Let People Know the Most Efficient Way to Reach You.

If you travel frequently or work in a time zone that is different from your main contacts, inform your colleagues how best to get in touch with you. How you decide to communicate will vary according to the other person's style. You may prefer to communicate with some people via e-mail because it is available 24 hours a day, while you may find a quick phone call or in-person chat more efficient with others. Let the nature and importance of your relationship dictate your mode of communication.

© Stop-Pressing-Snooze | Bill Hickie

59.   Always Be Interviewing.

The best way to be productive is to have a great team. So spend more time than most on human resources. Make sure your in touch with everyone. The top eight or ten people you're going to see automatically, but there are always twenty or thirty people who are up-and-comers or one or two levels down, and you want them to know you're paying attention. Intensive as all of this is, you ultimately save time, because you can delegate with confidence.

60.   Always Save Time to Exercise.

With the exception of one or two days a year, aim to work out every single day. Fitting a workout into the work day reduces stress, keeps you healthy, and is great for getting "alone time" to work out business and personal problems. When someone asks for a non-work-related meeting, see if they are up for doing the meeting while running or biking together. Work out at lunchtime.

61.   Schedule Time to Focus on the Big Picture.

A big part of productivity is being agile. Leave a lot of blocks in your day open. On an average day try to keep only 50 percent scheduled, though occasionally it may get as high as 80 percent. That's imperative, because often something comes up out of nowhere. If you have a free block and nothing presents itself, catch up on industry reports, self-education, and big-picture thinking. In a packed schedule, those things can get neglected. They shouldn't be.

© Stop-Pressing-Snooze | Bill Hickie

62.   Exercise your brain.

Brains, like bodies, need exercise to keep fit. If you don't exercise your brain, it will get flabby and useless. Exercise your brain by reading a lot, talking to clever people and disagreeing with people; arguing can be a terrific way to give your brain cells a workout.

                              | Bill Hickie

63.   Define Your Goals and Activities.

To feel nourished, energised and balanced, you need to define big-picture goals and activities for each category of your life. Many people set career or financial goals but neglect to set goals for other critical areas of their lives. If your life feels out of balance, think about where you are spending the majority of your time. Chances are that your time is being spent in those areas of your life for which your goals are clear-cut. For each of your major life or work categories, write down your big-picture goal. Consider your deepest values and ask yourself "What would make me happy in each of these key areas? What do I dream of attaining?". A goal is a destination. It's what you want to achieve. An activity is how you get there. It's the specific means to your higher goals. For example, "exercise three times per week" is not a goal. The question is why do you want to exercise? Perhaps it's to maximise your health. "Maximise my health" is a goal. Exercise is the activity that gets you there. Activities take up space in your schedule and can change from month to month and from year to year. Goals define the reward you are seeking. Big-picture goals are based on your core values, and they tend not to change much over the course of your life. For example, warm and loving relationships, well-adjusted children, financial security and wealth, expertise in a particular area, an inviting and comfortable home, and a sense of connection to your community are all values you are likely to hold onto throughout your life. Keep your big-picture goals simple and heartfelt. Once you know what your big-picture goals are, choose two or three specific activities that will help you achieve those goals. There are many ways to achieve any one big-picture goal.

                       | Bill Hickie

64.   Stop Fighting Fires.

The opposite of proactive is reactive. If you find yourself "fighting fires", or reacting to problems only after they crop up, take a good look at what is wrong!

65.   Strive for efficiency.

Be more efficient in everything you do. Find ways to eliminate, consolidate, shorten, quicken, and budget. That means budgeting your time, budgeting your money, and otherwise making the most of the resources at your disposal.

66.   Confidence is Key.

Be confident and project that confidence to others. Eventually, the people around you will start to believe you're going to achieve your goals. Eventually, many of those same doubters will find themselves trying to help you achieve your goals. Confidence is contagious. People want to achieve. People want to be on the winning side. So have confidence you're going to succeed.

| Bill Hickie

PART 3 - BEING MORE PRODUCTIVE

**"having the power of producing;
generative; creative"**

If you want to get more out of life strive to become more productive. When we think of productivity we normally think of a workplace contribution but productivity can apply to our hobbies and also to sport. When we talk about being more productive we are talking about getting more bang for your buck. In other words we want to get more or better work done in less time or with less effort.

The biggest key to productivity is organisation. The person who is organised will get more done in a shorter period of time. Productivity comes easily if you have a clear sense of what needs to accomplished each day and a plan to accomplish it. I found that when I listed the tasks that I needed to accomplish the next day and prioritised them work went very quickly. I had much more time left over at the end of the day to do whatever I deemed most necessary.

"Productivity is never an accident. It is always the result of a commitment to excellence, intelligent planning, and focused effort"

Paul J. Meyer

67.   Prioritise.

Rank Items on Your To-Do List. Make the next day's "to do" list before you leave the office. Rate each item A, B, or C based on its importance, and work on "A" items first.

68.   Make Meetings Work.

The productiveness of any meeting depends on the advance thought given to the agenda, and you should never leave a meeting without writing a follow-up list with each item assigned to one person. This is a must.

69.   Go outside.

All the big ideas are on the outside. You'll never have a creative idea at your desk.

70.   Shrink Your Mental Deadlines.

If you think something is going to take an hour, give yourself 40 minutes. By shrinking your mental deadlines, you work faster and with greater focus. Also a "Stop Doing" list is as important as a "To Do" list. A "To Do" list is easy, you just keep adding to it and the more you have on it, the more important you may feel. But "Stop Doing" is more difficult because you have to give up some things.

© Stop-Pressing-Snooze | Bill Hickie

71.   Avoid Multi-tasking.

Don't multitask. Multitasking is something we all do these days. The problem is our brains just aren't cut out for it. When you multitask, you're interfering with your brain's ability to perform at max-capacity. In most cases, multi-tasking = less-tasking. When you make those shifts from one context to another, you risk dropping things from your short-term memory. Do one thing at a time, minimize context shifts and maximise brain power.

72.   Think little and large.

Think of work as either large or little. The large work requires thinking and focus. Typically, large work involves the most significant clients and long-term commitments. The little work requires action and consists of emails, phone calls and virtually all administration. It also includes domestic administration. Large work makes money; little work organises it or spends it. Spend 80 percent of your day doing large work. The rest gets done between important activities, in the evening or when you are too tired to do anything that requires a lot of thought.

73.   Establish routine.

Try hard to establish routines and stick to them. The more you can do without thinking, the more effort is left for the work that counts. You don't want to think about how or when to get to work, have lunch or take the tube home. The more choices you eliminate from your day, the more time you have to focus on what's difficult and productive. In leadership positions, the hardest time to protect is pure thinking time.

74.　　Focus on Your Core Competencies.

Most people have "core competencies", the things that we do best and that other people can't do for us. Usually, these fall into three categories: nurturing careers, nurturing our family and close friends, and nurturing ourselves. For example, only you can focus on your long-term career development; only you can play with your kids or build a relationship with your partner; only you can sleep or exercise. And as for everything else that doesn't fit into those categories? Ignore, minimise or delegate.

75.　　Enjoy silence.

To avoid getting distracted by devices that are engineered specifically to take us away from what we're doing, we need to set everything to silence including, every once in a while, ourselves.

76.　　Cut Your Workday by 30 Minutes.

You will get more done. A deadline forces you to eliminate all the little time-wasters, silly interruptions, procrastination & perfectionism. Just because you can work all the time doesn't mean you should. Every now and then cut your workday by thirty minutes. Dedicate evenings and wherever possible weekends completely to your personal life and most importantly, your family.

77.   Define an Outcome for Every Meeting.

Identify a topic and outcome for every meeting, and send it to all participants a minimum of 24 hours beforehand so that everyone comes prepared. Well-run, useful meetings provide enormous value; they can solve problems, generate ideas, save you time, clarify direction, build teamwork, and reignite passion for projects.

78.   Reduce Paper Clutter.

Eighty percent of what is filed is never looked at again. Before saving any document, ask yourself whether you would trust that the information is up to date next time you look for it. If not, it's time to ditch, shred or recycle. For printing, use double sided printing to generate fewer pages. Only print the information you really need.

79.   Use E-mail to Document .

When scheduling travel and social activities, communicate plans through e-mail to both family and colleagues to keep an easy record of correspondence rather than relying on a possibly hurried conversation.

© Stop-Pressing-Snooze | Bill Hickie

80.   Create Templates.

There is no need to write from scratch every time. Whilst you don't want your correspondence to sound like a form letter, writing every letter from scratch is an enormous waste of time. Creating a template for every document that must be sent more than once opens up your schedule for other work. Just be sure to customise your template based on the contact to which you are writing.

81.   Set the Due Date.

No matter how much room you leave for creativity in the delegation process, never be vague about the due date. If you leave the due date vague, other priorities will attract your delegate's focus, or not leave you enough time to correct the work, if necessary. Leave enough of a cushion so that if the work doesn't come back as you'd hoped, there is enough time to correct it before the real deadline. It's sometimes helpful to give the person an estimate of how long you think the task should take and how long you want them to spend on it. Put a reminder in your planner to follow up the day the task is due.

82.   Turn It Off.

Technology is addictive, and answering and checking messages incessantly can drive impulsive behaviour and stress. You need to control the devices, instead of the other way around, to be able to bring full attention to your work and decisions and clear space for your life. Make sure you have daily disconnect time to remove yourself from the fray. Send less mail. Ask before you click: Is this message critical? Does it rise to the importance of a phone call? Are you sending the message because you can? Congratulate yourself on how many messages you resist sending each day.

83.   Get Organised.

Entrepreneurs are great at action and the big picture but not so good at keeping piles of junk at bay. Let go of stuff that's bogging you down and cluttering up your desk and thinking. File, act, or throw. Getting organised frees up clarity and vitality that can increase your performance for the tasks that are the most important and may be getting sidetracked by the jungle of low-priority chaos.

84.   Find a Shortcut.

When time is limited, you need to find the quickest way to your goal. Finding shortcuts is not about "cheating" or taking the easy way out; it's about becoming more efficient. It's usually preferable to have something completed (even if it's imperfect) than never done at all. For each item on your to-do list, ask yourself: Is there a quicker way to get this done? Skipping certain steps can shrink one-time projects.

85. Empower Your Subordinates.

Having a team that works for you can take a huge chunk off your workload if you delegate properly. However, if they do not feel confident in their roles, they will be unsure about the work they are doing. If you're supervising people, empower them to make decisions so you're not constantly inundated with tiny questions. Next time someone comes to you with a problem they could handle on their own, turn it back around. Try these responses: "Can you make that call? I won't be able to get to it for two days" or "Come up with a few solutions, and then let's meet and talk about them."

86. Don't Look to the Past During a Time of Change.

Looking to the past when the rest of the world is trying desperately to move forward prevents all involved from moving swiftly. You become the anchor, the weight, holding yourself and everyone else down. It may feel like an abrupt shifting of gears; but that's precisely what you have to do. During a time of change, you can't make assumptions. The old rules don't apply. Pay attention and stop interpreting things in relation to what used to be. Don't compare. Take in the new facts so you can respond to reality instead of your images of the good old days. Be willing to look forward and embrace new ideas.

87. Learn to Delegate.

Life starts coming back into the picture when you can trust enough to delegate. If you have good people, they will rise to the challenge, and that will free you up to do the important tasks and get time for a life outside the office. Take the time to train new people.

© Stop-Pressing-Snooze | Bill Hickie

88.   Create Focus Zones.

Nonstop interruptions can prevent you from having the space to concentrate on your most important tasks. Sometimes the only time you can get anything done is after everyone has gone home. That's a prescription for burnout and life-denial. Create a focus zone for yourself every day. Take an hour or two and block them off with no interruptions, and take care of your high-concentration work during this period. Most people find the first hour or two of the day the best time for focus zones.

89.   Archive Your E-mail.

Archive your e-mail every week. Doing so will save time later searching through thousands of e-mails in an inbox. Time spent doing this is well worth it.

90.   Make Use of Your Travel Time.

Whether commuting, shuttling your kids from one after-school activity to the next, or taking a business trip, make a conscious choice about how you want to use that travel time. Travel time should never be lost time. Choose the best mode of transportation for whatever you're planning to do. A cross-country car trip is a great way to build relationships; public transportation offers plenty of time to sleep (physical health), read or listen to music (escape), and concentrate (work).

© Stop-Pressing-Snooze | Bill Hickie

91.   Focus on the Joys of Completion.

There is a direct correlation between job satisfaction and achievement. People who accomplish a lot are driven by a certain joy of completion; the thrill of crossing things off their to-do list. It's often what keeps them focused when the going gets rough on a particular task. An adrenaline high gets triggered when things are finished. That sense of accomplishment is highly energising and keeps you tackling one task after another all day long.

92.   Just One More.

Lots of people have more work than they can get done in a given day, so it's easy to fall prey to the "just one more thing" syndrome. One more e-mail. One more call. Before you know it, it's 9 p.m. Keep yourself in check with stop times. Pick a day and choose a time when you will put the day's work to bed no matter what. At 6:30 p.m., you're done. Choose your stop times, and you can avoid defaulting to the "one more thing" syndrome and burnout.

93.   Set Rules for E-mail.

Receiving 100 e-mails a day is not unusual. That adds up to around 100 days a year doing nothing but reading and answering e-mail. The problem is that electronic messaging is unbounded. For optimal performance and a lot less stress and fewer interruptions, you have to set the rules of engagement. Create a list of interruption management rules that include manual checking of all messages at set times, limited reply and resisting the temptation to send unless it's important.

94.   Delegate One Big Job.

Knowing how to delegate effectively is one of the most important and valuable time management skills anyone can develop. Delegating tasks is not something you do to avoid your responsibilities; it's a technique you use to fulfil them. Moving tasks off your plate frees you up to focus your energies where you can make a unique contribution. It may not be in your nature to depend on anyone but you. Break the habit and the irrational belief that you are the only person who can do things right. It's time to discover that other people can offer fresh and unique ideas. Focus on the fact that, like you, most people are responsible and enjoy making a contribution. It can be difficult to know what to delegate, and how to do it in a way that saves, rather than costs, you time. One of the greatest benefits of delegation is that it promotes a healthy interdependence among people. Delegation isn't about burdening others but giving them a chance to make a contribution and provide value to the team.

© Stop-Pressing-Snooze | Bill Hickie

95. Create your own Gold Mine.

We are constantly in search of professional development. We attend seminars, industry conferences and trade shows, and along the way we amass a lot of information that can quickly turn into a disorganised mess. Learn how to select the most important information from all the papers you collect and apply it to your work. As you sift through all of your research and hand-outs, transfer all of the tips, facts and information that are new and useful onto a single sheet of paper or e-document then place the sheet or e-document in a folder named "Gold Mine". In addition to saving on storage, writing all those important points down has another benefit; It will help you retain the information, making you more likely to apply it.

96. Choose Paper or Electronic.

If you keep your calendar electronically but find yourself making appointments when you are at a meeting and scribbling them on paper, enter them on your computer as soon as you get back to your desk rather than relying on the written record. If your database of business contacts is held electronically and you collect a business card at a conference, enter that information in your computer and throw away the card. Alternatively, if you prefer to keep all phone numbers in an old-fashioned Rolodex, and someone e-mails you their phone or other contact information, automatically transfer it to your Rolodex. There should be just one place to look! If it's hard to motivate yourself to take the time to put things away, change your outlook. You're not putting things away; you're positioning them for their next use.

97.   Determine Your Concentration Threshold.

How long can you ignore all distractions and give 100 percent of your attention to one task? Ten minutes at a time? Thirty minutes? Two hours? Four hours? We each have a different concentration threshold. Find out what yours is. How long can you give one task your undivided attention before you begin to feel saturated, distracted or drawn towards taking care of something else? Study yourself; you may be surprised by what you learn. Once you know your threshold, begin to build up your tolerance. If you start at 10 minutes, add five minutes, then five more, and five more, increasing to 20, then 30 minutes. Your goal is being able to focus for a full hour. You'll be amazed how much you can actually get done in a full hour of complete focus.

98.   Create A Buffer Zone Between Work And Home.

To ease re-entry back into your personal life each night, you need to decompress from the day's pressure cooker. You've been in one mode all day; aggressive, competitive, objective-oriented; none of which works in your private life. Find a transitional space to bring the pressure down. Go to the gym, read, or find some calming space that can bring you back to life.

99.   Above all else, remember to enjoy life.

Happy people are productive people. If you are not happy, find out why and do something about it.

100.   Stop Pressing Snooze.

If you have read this far, then the rest is easy. All you have to do is remember three simple words that are the final tip, thereafter you'll know what to do.

"Stop-Pressing-Snooze"

| Bill Hickie

| Bill Hickie

Stop Pressing Snooze isn't just a book or a phrase; it's a way of life, a lifestyle choice.

At times whilst writing this book and compiling this collection of tips and tools my motivation and drive was tested...my resolve was stretched. Having the words "Stop Pressing Snooze" indelibly etched in my mind fuelled my desire to do exactly that.

Writing this book not only helped me to Stop Pressing Snooze, it enabled me to focus on what was really important in my life and establish a clear vision and set of goals. This vision, goals and associated values are what drive my very existence and forge my path through life.

I imagined this book, and turned that thought into a reality. That was possible because I had a real desire to do so, a visualisation of the end product, the path to get there and the stubborn, single-minded persistence that meant I would never give up. Most importantly, above all I believed in myself and had faith in my own ability to succeed. Three simple words can help you do the same.

"Stop Pressing Snooze"

Bill Hickie – 2014

| Bill Hickie

| Bill Hickie